New Zealand 2024 Travel Guide

Beyond the Hobbiton: Exploring New Zealand's Film and Fantasy Landscapes

Thomas Will

Thomas Will

Copyright ©2023 Thomas Will

All Rights Reserved

NEW ZEALAND 2024 TRAVEL GUIDE

CHAPTER 1 — 6

Introduction — 6
- Welcome to Middle-earth: Overview of New Zealand's Film Connections — 6
- A Brief History of Filming in New Zealand — 6
- New Zealand as a Cinematic Playground — 7
- From Frodo to the Silver Screen: The Influence of "The Lord of the Rings" — 8

CHAPTER 2 — 10

Getting There — 10
- The Journey to Middle-earth: Travel Tips and Practical Information — 10
- Flights to New Zealand's Major Cities — 10
- Airport Transfers and Transportation Options — 13
- Visa Requirements and Border Crossings — 15

CHAPTER 3 — 18

Hobbiton and Beyond — 18
- Hobbiton: A Magical Encounter — 18
- Guided Tours of Hobbiton — 18
- Film Set Locations in Matamata — 20
- Tips for Visiting the Shire — 22
- Exploring Other Film Locations — 23
- Rivendell: The Elven Realm — 25

CHAPTER 4 — 27

Film Fanatic's Accommodation — 27
- Where to Rest Your Feet After a Day of Adventure — 27
- Hobbit Holes and Themed Accommodations — 27
- Cozy Lodges and Boutique Hotels — 29
- Hostels and Budget-Friendly Stays — 31
- Staying in Film-Friendly Locations — 34
- Conclusion: Your Cinematic Journey Continues — 35

CHAPTER 5 — 36

Satisfying Your Inner Foodie — 36
- Culinary Adventures in Film-Themed Settings — 36
- Hobbiton Feast: Dining in the Shire — 36
- Themed Cafes and Restaurants — 38
- Wellington's Creative Haven: "The Weta Cave Workshop & Café" — 39
- Auckland's Rooftop Wonderland: "The Glass Goose Bar & Eatery" — 40
- Tasting New Zealand's Film-Inspired Dishes — 41

CHAPTER 6 — 43

Fantasy-Infused Activities — 43
- Beyond Film Sets: Adventure Awaits — 43
- Outdoor Adventures in Middle-earth — 43
- Hiking the Tongariro Alpine Crossing — 46
- Exploring Fiordland National Park — 48
- Skydiving Over Remarkable Mountains — 50
- Cultural Experiences for Fantasy Lovers — 52
- Maori Cultural Performances — 55
- Traditional Maori Workshops — 57
- Nightlife in Fantasy-Themed Bars — 60

CHAPTER 7 — 64

Safety and Practical Tips — 64
- Navigating Middle-earth Safely — 64
- Local Customs and Cultural Sensitivities — 64
- Health Concerns and Vaccinations — 65
- Safety Concerns and Emergency Contacts — 66
- Weather and Climate Information — 67

CHAPTER 8 — 69

Conclusion — 69
- Your Journey Through New Zealand's Film and Fantasy Landscapes — 69

Capturing the Magic: Creating Lasting Memories					69

Thomas Will

DISCLAIMER

This travel guidebook doesn't contain any pictorial representation of any places described in it. This is done to retain authenticity of the writer and to avoid providing images that may unknowingly be copyrighted to another author. Also, the author wants the reader to be curious enough to visit the described places for an experience.

NEW ZEALAND 2024 TRAVEL GUIDE

Chapter 1

Introduction

Welcome to Middle-earth: Overview of New Zealand's Film Connections

New Zealand, a land of breathtaking natural beauty, has also carved a unique niche for itself in the world of cinema. It's not just a destination; it's a living, breathing film set that has played host to some of the most iconic movies in cinematic history. In this chapter, we'll embark on a journey that takes us beyond the ordinary, into the realms of fantasy and imagination that have been brought to life on New Zealand's picturesque landscapes.

A Brief History of Filming in New Zealand

To understand the cinematic allure of New Zealand, one must delve into its rich history of filmmaking. While New Zealand's film industry has grown exponentially over the years, it truly gained international recognition with the epic "The Lord of the Rings" trilogy directed by Peter Jackson. These films, adapted from J.R.R. Tolkien's novels, showcased the country's stunning landscapes and forever etched Middle-earth into the hearts of moviegoers worldwide. Since then, New Zealand has been a sought-after location for filmmakers seeking unparalleled natural beauty.

The early days of filmmaking in New Zealand were characterized by the production of local documentaries and short films. However, it wasn't until the late 1970s that the country began to gain attention on the global stage. One of the first international successes was Roger Donaldson's "Sleeping Dogs" (1977), a film that highlighted New Zealand's rugged landscapes and introduced the world to its unique cinematic potential.

Throughout the 1980s and early 1990s, New Zealand continued to make its mark on the film industry. Jane Campion's "The Piano" (1993) won the Palme d'Or at the Cannes Film Festival, bringing global acclaim to New Zealand talent. However, it was Peter Jackson's vision of Middle-earth that truly catapulted the country to fame.

New Zealand as a Cinematic Playground

What makes New Zealand a filmmaker's dream destination? The answer lies in its astounding variety of landscapes, ranging from snow-capped mountains to lush forests, pristine beaches to otherworldly volcanic terrain. It's a land of contrasts, where you can find rolling farmlands, dense rainforests, and geothermal wonders—all within a few hours' drive. This diversity allows filmmakers to recreate a wide array of settings, from the idyllic Shire to the foreboding slopes of Mount Doom.

New Zealand's cinematic appeal extends beyond its landscapes. The country boasts a talented pool of actors, directors, and crew members who have contributed to the success of numerous films and television series. The local film industry continues to thrive, fostering innovation and creativity.

From Frodo to the Silver Screen: The Influence of "The Lord of the Rings"

"The Lord of the Rings" not only put New Zealand on the cinematic map but also had a profound influence on the nation's tourism industry. Fans of the franchise, affectionately known as "Ringers," flock to New Zealand year-round to walk in the footsteps of Frodo and Gandalf. The film's enduring legacy can be seen in the meticulous preservation of Hobbiton, the Shire's charming village. Visitors can explore the hobbit holes, lush gardens, and even enjoy a pint at the Green Dragon Inn.

Beyond "The Lord of the Rings," New Zealand has continued to be a favored destination for filmmakers worldwide. "The Chronicles of Narnia," "Avatar," "The Hobbit," and "The Piano" are just a few of the other notable films shot against New Zealand's captivating backdrop. Each film has left its mark on the country, with dedicated tours and experiences allowing travelers to step into the cinematic worlds created on these shores.

As we embark on this cinematic adventure through New Zealand, prepare to be enchanted by the same landscapes that inspired filmmakers and transported audiences to fantastical realms. In the following chapters, we will explore the film sets, accommodations, cuisine, activities, and practical tips for a journey through New Zealand's film and fantasy landscapes. Whether you're a dedicated fan or simply seeking the magic of this unique destination, our guide will be your trusty companion on this extraordinary expedition.

Chapter 2

Getting There

The Journey to Middle-earth: Travel Tips and Practical Information

New Zealand, with its enchanting film and fantasy landscapes, beckons travelers from around the world. To embark on this epic cinematic adventure, you need to navigate the journey smoothly. In this chapter, we'll provide you with essential travel tips and practical information to ensure your voyage to Middle-earth is as seamless as possible.

Flights to New Zealand's Major Cities

Your journey to New Zealand is the commencement of an extraordinary adventure, and it all begins with selecting the right flight. New Zealand boasts several international airports, with Auckland, Wellington, and Christchurch standing out as the primary gateways to this captivating land. Each of these airports offers its unique charm and access to different parts of this breathtaking country.

Auckland Airport: Auckland Airport, nestled on the North Island, stands as the nation's busiest aviation hub. It not only caters to a vast number of international travelers but also offers the most extensive array of flight options. As you disembark at Auckland Airport, you're greeted by the warm embrace of New Zealand's North Island, promising diverse experiences, from vibrant cityscapes to serene beaches and cultural encounters.

Wellington Airport: **Serving as the capital of New Zealand, Wellington Airport provides a gateway to the enchanting landscapes of the North Island. This airport offers a seamless transition into the heart of the nation's governance and culture. As you arrive at Wellington Airport, you'll discover a city brimming with artistic vibrancy, culinary delights, and access to picturesque natural wonders.**

Christchurch Airport: **Located on the South Island, Christchurch Airport welcomes travelers with open arms to explore the island's remarkable natural wonders. Nestled amidst stunning landscapes, this airport provides an entry point to the breathtaking scenery that defines the South Island. As you step onto the tarmac at Christchurch Airport, you're enveloped by the allure of snow-capped mountains, pristine lakes, and outdoor adventures awaiting your discovery.**

When embarking on your flight to New Zealand, consider various factors that can enhance your travel experience:

1. *Airline Selection:* Choose an airline that aligns with your preferences and travel priorities. From luxurious carriers to budget-friendly options, you'll find a range of choices to suit your needs.

2. *Layover Options:* Depending on your departure city and airline choice, you may encounter layovers during your journey. Consider whether you'd like to explore a connecting city or prefer a direct flight to your final destination.

3. *Departure City:* New Zealand is accessible from numerous international hubs around the world. Selecting a departure city that suits your convenience and travel plans can streamline your journey.

4. *Direct Flights:* Direct flights to New Zealand are available from various international hubs, ensuring a convenient and efficient travel experience. These flights eliminate the need for layovers and offer a seamless journey to your chosen gateway.

As you embark on this remarkable journey to New Zealand, the selection of your flight is the first step towards immersing yourself in the cinematic landscapes, cultural richness, and outdoor adventures that await. Your adventure in Middle-earth begins with the anticipation of the skies, and with each mile, you draw closer to a world of wonder and enchantment.

Airport Transfers and Transportation Options

Your arrival in New Zealand marks the beginning of your immersive journey into the enchanting realms of film and fantasy. To ensure a seamless transition from the airport to your desired destinations, New Zealand offers a well-organized and efficient transportation network, ensuring that your adventure begins without a hitch.

Airport Transfer Options: **New Zealand's major airports provide a range of convenient options to transfer from the airport to your chosen film and fantasy locations. These options typically include:**

Taxis: **Taxis are a reliable and convenient means of transportation from the airport to your destination. Taxi stands are readily available at airports, and friendly drivers are there to assist you.**

Shuttle Services: **Shuttle services are a popular choice, particularly for travelers heading to hotels or** accommodations in specific areas. They offer shared rides, ensuring cost-effectiveness and convenience.

Rental Cars: If you prefer the freedom of exploring at your own pace, rental car agencies at the airports provide a range of vehicle options. Having your own vehicle grants you the flexibility to embark on spontaneous adventures and explore off-the-beaten-path locations.

Public Transportation: Auckland and Wellington boast efficient public transportation networks that connect the airports to various parts of the city and beyond. These options may include buses and trains, allowing you to easily explore the surrounding areas.

City Transport: Within the cities, you'll find a host of convenient transportation options:

Buses: Public buses operate on comprehensive routes, making it easy to navigate the city and visit nearby attractions.

Trains: Auckland and Wellington offer commuter train services that are not only efficient but also scenic, providing a unique way to explore the urban landscapes.

Ride-Sharing Services: **In many New Zealand cities, ride-sharing services like Uber are widely available. These services offer another convenient and comfortable option for getting around, especially for shorter trips or when you prefer door-to-door service.**

Information Resources: **To ensure you have the most up-to-date information on transportation options and prices, consider checking the official websites of the airports you'll be arriving at or inquire at information desks within the terminals. Airport staff and attendants are usually well-informed and ready to assist you in making the best transportation choices based on your needs and preferences.**

As you touch down in New Zealand and begin your adventure through film and fantasy landscapes, the efficient and varied transportation options at your disposal ensure that every step of your journey is as memorable and hassle-free as the destination itself. Your exploration of Middle-earth is within reach, and the journey promises to be as extraordinary as the sights and experiences that await.

Visa Requirements and Border Crossings

Before embarking on your epic journey to Middle-earth, it's crucial to navigate New Zealand's visa requirements and border crossing procedures. New Zealand provides a range of visa types based on your nationality, the purpose of your visit, and the duration of your stay, ensuring that travelers from across the world can explore this cinematic wonderland.

Visa Types: **New Zealand's visa landscape is diverse. Visa-exempt travelers from select countries can enjoy a visa-free stay of up to 90 days. However, others may need to apply for a visitor visa in advance. To ensure you meet the correct requirements, it's essential to consult the New Zealand Immigration website or contact the nearest New Zealand embassy or consulate. This step is vital to ascertain the specific visa requirements that apply to your unique travel circumstances.**

Visitor Visa: **If you do require a visitor visa, the process typically involves submitting an application, providing supporting documentation, and possibly attending an interview at a New Zealand embassy or consulate. Visitor visas are often granted for tourism, visiting family and friends, or other non-business-related activities.**

Border Control Procedures: **Upon arrival in New Zealand, you'll navigate customs and border control procedures to gain entry. New Zealand upholds strict biosecurity regulations to safeguard its distinctive ecosystems. To** ensure a hassle-free experience at the border, keep the following in mind:

Declaration: **Declare any food, plant, or animal products you're carrying in your luggage. New Zealand's biosecurity measures are stringent, and adherence to declaration requirements is essential to prevent any complications at the border.**

Customs Guidelines: **Familiarize yourself with New Zealand's customs guidelines and rules regarding items you can and cannot bring into the country. This awareness will assist you in packing and organizing your belongings appropriately.**

By arming yourself with knowledge about New Zealand's visa requirements and border crossing procedures, you'll ensure a seamless entry into the realm of cinematic wonders. With these logistical details well in hand, you can focus your attention on the extraordinary film and fantasy experiences that await in New Zealand, where every corner of the landscape seems touched by the magic of Middle-earth.

In the following chapters, we'll delve deeper into the film sets, accommodations, dining options, and activities that will make your journey through Middle-earth truly unforgettable.

Chapter 3

Hobbiton and Beyond

Hobbiton: A Magical Encounter

Prepare to step into the enchanting world of hobbits as we explore the iconic Hobbiton film set, one of New Zealand's most beloved cinematic treasures. Nestled in the heart of the North Island, Matamata, this meticulously crafted village brings J.R.R. Tolkien's vision to life, and it's a must-visit for any fan of "The Lord of the Rings."

Guided Tours of Hobbiton

Your immersion into the world of Hobbiton begins with a guided tour that is nothing short of a magical journey. These tours promise to transport you to the heart of the Shire, where the delightful charm of this fantasy realm comes to life. Led by knowledgeable guides, who often don hobbit attire themselves, the experience is nothing short of enchanting.

Enchanted Guides: Your adventure commences with guides who are not just well-versed in the lore of Hobbiton but who also embrace the spirit of hobbits. They often don the iconic attire of the Shire's inhabitants, complete with vests, suspenders, and perhaps a hint of whimsy in their step. Their warm and jovial presence creates an instant connection to the magical world you're about to explore.

The Lush Landscape: **As you step into Hobbiton, you find yourself surrounded by a lush and picturesque landscape. The rolling hills are dotted with charming hobbit holes, vibrant gardens, and quirky details that add a palpable sense of wonder to the experience. The Shire's beauty unfolds before you, every step a revelation, every sight a marvel.**

Familiar Film Locations: **Your guided journey brings you face to face with familiar locations from the films. The famous Bag End, the Hobbiton residence of Bilbo and Frodo Baggins, stands as a testament to the meticulous attention to detail. The Green Dragon Inn, a hub of hobbit merriment, beckons you to step inside and experience the conviviality that was shared by hobbits. And the Party Tree, a symbol of celebrations in the Shire, stands with its branches spread wide in welcome. It's not just the major landmarks; every corner and crevice of Hobbiton exudes authenticity, making it a truly magical experience.**

Living Authenticity: **The enchantment of Hobbiton lies in its authenticity. The little details are what truly make** this place extraordinary. Smoke lazily rising from the chimneys, laundry gently swaying in the breeze, and freshly tended gardens add to the illusion that you have indeed stepped into a living, breathing hobbit village. The charm of Hobbiton is in the details, from the cobblestone pathways to the intricately crafted window shutters.

With each step, you traverse through this enchanting village, where fantasy and reality intertwine seamlessly. The magic of Hobbiton isn't confined to the movies; it's alive and thriving in the meticulously recreated landscape, beckoning you to become a part of its timeless tale. This guided tour is your key to unlocking the doors of imagination and stepping into a world where hobbits, wizards, and epic adventures await around every corner.

Film Set Locations in Matamata

While Hobbiton undeniably steals the spotlight, Matamata unveils a treasure trove of film set locations, inviting you to dive deeper into the cinematic magic. Beyond the iconic hobbit holes, this enchanting region offers a sprawling canvas of picturesque farmlands and rolling hills that once served as captivating backdrops for various scenes in Middle-earth.

Beyond the Hobbit Holes: **As you meander beyond the charming hobbit holes, a world of cinematic wonder unfolds. The landscape around Matamata is a testament to New Zealand's natural beauty, and it's no wonder that it was chosen to bring Middle-earth to life. The panoramic vistas, vibrant greenery, and gentle slopes of the land transport you into the heart of this fantastical realm.**

Mill Farm: **One of the remarkable film set locations in Matamata is the enchanting Mill Farm, a site that played a pivotal role in "The Hobbit" trilogy. The serene and idyllic beauty of this location is enough to take your breath away. Here, you're not merely observing a backdrop; you're stepping into the very scenes where epic tales of heroism and adventure were filmed.**

Captivating Views: **Mill Farm offers not just an escape into a world of imagination but also captivating views of the surrounding countryside. The rolling hills extend as far as the eye can see, dappled with the vibrant hues of New Zealand's lush countryside. The play of light and shadow on the landscape creates a mesmerizing panorama that lingers in your memory long after you've departed.**

Rural Charm: **As you explore Matamata's film set locations, you'll encounter the authentic rural charm of**

New Zealand's countryside. The quaint charm of farms, the gentle sway of tall grass in the breeze, and the sense of tranquility envelop you. You're not merely visiting a movie set; you're immersing yourself in a genuine New Zealand rural experience.

Matamata's film set locations extend an open invitation to all those who seek to explore beyond the hobbit holes and embark on a journey that captures the very essence of Middle-earth. With each step you take on this cinematic pilgrimage, you traverse landscapes that have witnessed the creation of epic tales, making the magic of the movies a tangible reality.

Tips for Visiting the Shire

To make the most of your visit to Hobbiton and Matamata, here are some valuable tips:

Book in Advance: Hobbiton tours are highly popular, so it's advisable to book your tickets in advance to secure your spot.

Photography: Don't forget your camera! You'll want to capture every magical moment in the Shire.

Green Dragon Inn: Conclude your tour with a visit to the Green Dragon Inn, where you can enjoy a complimentary beverage. Try the specially brewed Hobbiton Ale or Southfarthing Range of beverages.

Souvenirs: **The Shire's Rest, the tour's starting point, has a charming gift shop with unique souvenirs and Middle-earth memorabilia.**

Respect the Environment: **Help preserve the beauty of Hobbiton by respecting the rules and guidelines provided by your tour guide.**

Exploring Other Film Locations

Beyond the enchanting embrace of the Shire, New Zealand extends an invitation to explore a diverse array of stunning film locations that have played pivotal roles in various cinematic adventures. These landscapes, though distinct from the rolling hills of Hobbiton, boast their own unique allure, each contributing its magic to the realm of Middle-earth.

The Remarkables - Misty Mountains: **Journey to the Remarkables, a striking mountain range situated near Queenstown, and you'll find yourself amidst the very Misty Mountains depicted in "The Hobbit." The rugged, snow-capped peaks and the wilderness that unfolds at their feet create a dramatic and awe-inspiring landscape. Every twist and turn in these mountains is a** photographer's dream, offering a canvas for capturing the majesty and mystique of Middle-earth.

Wellington - The Heart of Film: Wellington, the capital of New Zealand, is not only a thriving metropolis but also a bustling hub of cinematic wonder. It's home to Weta Workshop, the creative genius behind the creatures, props, and visual effects that brought Middle-earth to life on the big screen. Here, the boundaries of imagination know no limits. You can explore the Weta Cave, a window into the enchanting world of movie magic, where you'll encounter an array of props and memorabilia that will transport you to the heart of the films.

Behind-the-Scenes Tours: For the true aficionado of cinematic artistry, Wellington offers behind-the-scenes tours of Weta Workshop and other film-related activities. You'll gain firsthand insight into the meticulous craftsmanship that goes into the creation of movie magic, from the sculpting of characters to the construction of epic sets. The stories shared by the passionate artisans themselves add an extra layer of depth to your appreciation of the craft.

Immerse Yourself in Film Production: To truly immerse yourself in the artistry of film production, Wellington provides unique opportunities. From visiting film studios and witnessing live sets to exploring the creative processes of makeup and visual effects, every moment spent here is an invitation to step into the world of storytelling on screen.

These captivating film locations beyond the Shire are a testament to the breadth and depth of New Zealand's cinematic contributions. Each one, whether a mountain range, a bustling city, or a workshop of creative genius, adds a layer to the grand tapestry of Middle-earth. As you explore these sites, you'll discover that the magic of film extends far beyond the confines of the cinema screen, becoming a tangible reality that you can touch, see, and experience in every corner of this remarkable land.

Rivendell: The Elven Realm

Your journey through New Zealand's film and fantasy landscapes wouldn't be complete without a visit to Rivendell, the mystical elven realm from "The Lord of the Rings." Located in Kaitoke Regional Park, just a short drive from Wellington, Rivendell captures the ethereal beauty of Tolkien's world. Take a leisurely walk through lush forest trails, where you'll find plaques with film quotes and scenes that transport you to this enchanting realm.

As you explore Rivendell, it's impossible not to be captivated by the tranquility of the surroundings and the sense of wonder that the films evoked. The location perfectly embodies the magic of New Zealand's film connections, allowing you to connect with the heart of Middle-earth.

In the upcoming chapters, we'll delve into accommodation options, dining experiences, and outdoor adventures that will complete your cinematic journey through New Zealand. Whether you're an avid film buff or simply seeking the beauty of these picturesque landscapes, your adventure in Middle-earth continues to unfold.

Chapter 4

Film Fanatic's Accommodation

Where to Rest Your Feet After a Day of Adventure

After a day of immersing yourself in New Zealand's cinematic wonders, you'll want a comfortable and unique place to rest your weary feet. In this chapter, we'll explore a range of accommodation options that cater to film fanatics and provide a cozy haven amidst the captivating landscapes.

Hobbit Holes and Themed Accommodations

For the most enchanting and film-inspired experience, consider taking your stay in New Zealand to the next level by residing in a genuine hobbit hole or themed accommodation. Several providers across the country offer these cozy and charming hobbit-style lodgings, creating an experience that transcends ordinary travel and transports you straight into the heart of the Shire.

Genuine Hobbit Holes: **These accommodations faithfully recreate the iconic hobbit holes that dot the landscape of Hobbiton. With round doors and earthy interiors that mimic the warm, inviting aesthetics of the Shire, these lodgings provide an immersive experience that is truly** one of a kind. The attention to detail is remarkable, and each stay is an opportunity to live like a hobbit, if only for a little while.

Modern Comforts: **While the charm of these accommodations lies in their authentic design, you won't have to forgo modern comforts. Most hobbit holes and themed lodgings come equipped with the amenities you need for a comfortable stay. From cozy bedding to private bathrooms, you can enjoy the best of both worlds – the rustic allure of the Shire and the convenience of contemporary living.**

Surrounded by Serenity: **Picture waking up in your very own hobbit hole, the tranquil New Zealand countryside spreading out before you. The idyllic landscapes, from rolling hills to lush pastures, create a serene backdrop that is a feast for the senses. It's not just a stay; it's an escape into a world where nature and fantasy are intertwined.**

Themed Meals and Activities: **Many providers go the extra mile to ensure your stay is truly immersive. They offer themed meals that take inspiration from the Shire's cuisine, from hearty second breakfasts to delicious suppers. Activities, such as guided tours of film locations or hobbit-themed events, add an extra layer of enchantment to your stay. You might find yourself** sharing stories and songs just as hobbits do or embarking on your own epic adventure in the surrounding landscapes.

Staying in a hobbit hole or themed accommodation in New Zealand is a chance to transform your trip into an extraordinary and unforgettable adventure. It's an opportunity to live out your own Middle-earth story, surrounded by the beauty of New Zealand's countryside and the magic of the films. It's an experience that transcends the boundaries of ordinary travel and allows you to become a part of the cinematic wonder that is New Zealand.

Cozy Lodges and Boutique Hotels

New Zealand offers a treasure trove of lodges and boutique hotels that harmonize luxury and natural beauty in a way that is both comforting and captivating. Nestled within the embrace of stunning landscapes, these accommodations beckon as a tranquil haven after a day of exploration. What sets these lodges and hotels apart is their commitment to ensuring your stay feels like a genuine escape, where comfort and the splendors of nature converge.

Tranquil Retreats: **These lodges and boutique hotels are artfully situated amidst New Zealand's captivating landscapes. They provide a serene and peaceful retreat,** where you can relax and rejuvenate in an environment that exudes natural beauty. From pristine lakeshores to secluded forested nooks, each location is a gateway to both adventure and serenity.

Personalized Service: **One** hallmark of these accommodations is their dedication to personalized service. Here, your comfort is a top priority. Attentive staff members go the extra mile to ensure your needs are met, and your stay is tailored to your preferences. From personalized welcome amenities to concierge services, you'll feel that your every wish is their command.

Fine Dining Experiences: **The** dining experiences at these lodges and boutique hotels are nothing short of exceptional. The cuisine often celebrates local flavors, featuring fresh ingredients and innovative culinary creations. Dining here is not just a meal; it's an exploration of New Zealand's gastronomic heritage, often accompanied by stunning views of the surrounding landscapes.

Breathtaking Views: **The** views from these accommodations are often a highlight in themselves. Whether it's overlooking a pristine lake, gazing upon snow-capped mountains, or being enveloped by lush forests, the scenery that unfolds outside your window is a sight to behold. Every room is a front-row seat to the grandeur of New Zealand's natural beauty.

Diverse Options: The array of choices in New Zealand's lodging offerings is as diverse as its landscapes. You can opt for a secluded lodge deep in the wilderness, where you're embraced by the wild beauty of the land. Alternatively, you might choose a boutique hotel in a charming town, where you can immerse yourself in local culture and explore the area's unique attractions. Whether you're a seeker of solitude or a lover of vibrant communities, New Zealand's accommodations have something to offer every traveler.

In these cozy lodges and boutique hotels, you'll discover that your New Zealand experience is not merely about a place to rest your head; it's about an environment that enriches your journey. It's about finding your own slice of paradise within a paradise, where the comforts of home meet the splendor of nature. These accommodations are a testament to the art of living well, and they invite you to savor every moment of your New Zealand adventure.

Hostels and Budget-Friendly Stays

For travelers seeking to make the most of their budget while exploring New Zealand's wonders, the country offers a wide array of affordable accommodation options. Hostels stand out as a popular choice for backpackers and those mindful of their expenditures. They provide dormitory-style rooms, communal areas for mingling, and a unique opportunity to connect with fellow adventurers from every corner of the globe.

Affordability Meets Adventure: **Hostels are renowned for their affordability, allowing you to stretch your budget further while still enjoying comfortable lodging. These establishments are often located in prime locations, providing easy access to the country's most exciting attractions.**

Community and Camaraderie: **The communal environment of hostels encourages social interaction. Shared living spaces, common kitchens, and organized activities create an atmosphere where fellow travelers become instant friends. Exchanging stories, making plans, and sharing adventures are all part of the hostel experience.**

Diverse Options: **New Zealand's hostels come in a variety of styles to suit different preferences. Whether you opt for a laid-back beachfront hostel or one nestled within a vibrant city, there's a hostel that matches your travel style. Private rooms are also available for those seeking a bit more solitude.**

Holiday Parks for Budget-Seekers: **If you're on a quest for budget-friendly lodging that allows you to immerse yourself in New Zealand's natural beauty, holiday parks are a fantastic choice. These parks provide an assortment of options, including cozy cabins, campsites, and spaces for camper vans. Often, these parks are situated in scenic settings, allowing you to experience the splendor of the great outdoors without breaking the bank.**

Natural Beauty on a Budget: **Holiday parks provide a cost-effective way to enjoy New Zealand's stunning landscapes. Whether you're nestled in a forested paradise, perched near a serene lake, or camped on the coast, the affordability of these sites ensures that you don't have to compromise on experiencing the breathtaking beauty of the country.**

Adventure for All: **The beauty of New Zealand is that it welcomes travelers of all budgets. Hostels and holiday parks open doors to adventurers who seek to explore the country without the constraints of high costs. Here, the focus is on the experiences, the camaraderie of fellow travelers, and the thrill of discovering new horizons.**

In these budget-friendly accommodations, you'll find that New Zealand's adventure is accessible to all.

Whether you choose the social dynamics of a hostel or the tranquility of a holiday park, you'll discover that your budget need not limit your experiences. New Zealand's landscape is a treasure trove that welcomes travelers of all walks of life, and in these lodging options, you'll find the means to uncover it all.

Staying in Film-Friendly Locations

If you're keen on staying in film-friendly locations, consider accommodations in Wellington, Matamata, and Queenstown. These areas have strong ties to the film industry and offer lodging options that provide a sense of cinematic immersion.

Wellington, known as "Wellywood," is home to several film-related attractions and accommodations. From boutique hotels to cozy bed-and-breakfasts, you'll find a range of places to stay while exploring the city's film culture.

Matamata, the gateway to Hobbiton, offers accommodations that allow you to extend your magical Shire experience. Stay in charming cottages or lodges that provide easy access to the film set.

Queenstown, with its stunning mountain landscapes, is a popular choice for adventurers and film enthusiasts. The town offers a variety of accommodations, including luxury resorts, cozy lodges, and budget-friendly hostels.

As you plan your stay in New Zealand, consider the location that aligns with your film-related interests and the experiences you seek. Each region has its unique charm and cinematic connections waiting to be explored.

Conclusion: Your Cinematic Journey Continues

As you settle into your chosen accommodation, you'll feel a sense of anticipation for the adventures that await you. New Zealand's film and fantasy landscapes are not confined to the screen; they are a living, breathing testament to the magic of cinema.

In the upcoming chapters, we'll delve into the culinary delights of Middle-earth, the outdoor adventures that beckon, and the cultural experiences that allow you to immerse yourself in the heart of this cinematic world. Whether you're a dedicated film fanatic or simply seeking the beauty of these picturesque landscapes, your journey through New Zealand's film and fantasy realms continues to unfold.

Prepare to feast on delectable cuisine, embark on thrilling outdoor escapades, and immerse yourself in the captivating culture of New Zealand. Your cinematic journey is about to reach new heights, and the magic of Middle-earth awaits your discovery. So, dear traveler, the adventure is far from over. Get ready to embrace the wonders that await you in this extraordinary land of film and fantasy.

Chapter 5

Satisfying Your Inner Foodie

Culinary Adventures in Film-Themed Settings

New Zealand's culinary scene is as diverse as its landscapes, offering a delightful fusion of flavors that cater to every palate. In this chapter, we'll explore the culinary adventures that await you in film-themed settings, where you can savor the magic of Middle-earth while satisfying your inner foodie.

Hobbiton Feast: Dining in the Shire

Your cinematic journey through Middle-earth reaches its zenith when you embark on a culinary adventure fit for a hobbit. Within the enchanting confines of Hobbiton, where every corner exudes the essence of fantasy, you have the exclusive opportunity to dine just as Frodo and Bilbo Baggins would have. The Green Dragon Inn, with its cozy atmosphere and rustic charm, is where this delectable Shire-inspired dining experience comes to life.

A Shire-Inspired Culinary Adventure: As you step into the Green Dragon Inn, it's as if you've crossed over into the pages of J.R.R. Tolkien's novels. The warm glow of the hearth, the inviting wooden beams, and the merriment of fellow travelers envelop you in a sense of homely comfort. It's an atmosphere that's designed to transport you into the heart of the Shire, where good food and good company are cherished above all.

The Menu of Shire Delights: **The menu at the Green Dragon Inn is a love letter to the rich culinary traditions of the Shire. Hearty and flavorful, the dishes served here evoke the very spirit of hobbit feasting. One glance at the menu, and you'll find yourself torn between delectable choices. Will it be the "Hobbiton Beef and Ale Pie," a savory creation that's as comforting as a warm hearth on a cold day? Or perhaps you'll opt for "Samwise Gamgee's Slow-Roasted Pork Belly," a dish so tender and succulent that it's as if it's been prepared by a hobbit in the heart of the Shire.**

Specially Brewed Delights: **The experience doesn't stop at the food; the beverages served here are equally enchanting. You can pair your meal with a mug of "Hobbiton Ale," specially brewed to capture the earthy flavors that define the Shire. Alternatively, savor the crisp and refreshing "Sackville Cider," a beverage that embodies the wholesome essence of hobbit life. Each sip is a journey through the rolling hills and fertile fields of this fantasy realm.**

Merriment and Memory-Making: **Dining at the Green Dragon Inn isn't just about satisfying your appetite; it's about creating lasting memories. It's about sharing laughter and stories with your fellow travelers, just as hobbits would after a long day's adventure. The Green Dragon Inn's rustic charm and the delectable creations from its kitchen combine to create an experience that's both magical and heartwarming.**

Dining in the Shire at the Green Dragon Inn is a journey into the heart of hobbit culture. It's a culinary adventure that's as rich in flavors as it is in tradition. It's a chance to savor the simple pleasures and robust delights of hobbit life while creating memories that will linger like the aroma of freshly baked bread in the Shire's rolling hills.

Themed Cafes and Restaurants

The enchantment of cinema doesn't end with Hobbiton; it extends throughout New Zealand in the form of themed cafes and restaurants, each an homage to the world of film. Here, you can dine in surroundings that pay tribute to the magic of the movies, offering a culinary experience that's as delightful as it is immersive.

Wellington's Creative Haven: "The Weta Cave Workshop & Café"

Wellington, a city known for its artistic spirit, is home to a unique dining experience that's a cinematic feast for the senses. "The Weta Cave Workshop & Café" is more than just a place to enjoy a coffee or a meal; it's a celebration of the creative genius of Weta Workshop, the imaginative force behind some of cinema's most iconic creations.

A Culinary Journey Amongst Artifacts: **As you enter this exceptional establishment, you're surrounded by an array of props, sculptures, and memorabilia from beloved films. The ambiance is one of artistic wonder, where you can dine alongside iconic artifacts, and it's not unusual to find yourself in the company of beloved characters like Gollum, Trolls, and fantastical creatures.**

Savoring Creative Inspiration: **Dining here is akin to savoring creative inspiration with every bite. The menu is designed to be as artistic as the surroundings, offering dishes that are as visually stunning as they are flavorful. Whether you choose a light lunch or a hearty meal, each dish carries with it the spirit of cinematic artistry.**

Auckland's Rooftop Wonderland: "The Glass Goose Bar & Eatery"

In Auckland, "The Glass Goose Bar & Eatery" offers a dining experience that is elevated in more ways than one. Perched amidst the city skyline, this rooftop bar combines panoramic views with a cinematic touch that's sure to delight both film enthusiasts and foodies.

A Rooftop with a Star Wars Surprise: **The highlight of this rooftop gem is the life-sized AT-AT Walker from "Star Wars." As you savor your meal or enjoy a drink, you can't help but feel a sense of cinematic wonder as you gaze upon this iconic machine. The Auckland skyline and the AT-AT Walker are a match made in cinematic heaven, creating a backdrop that's both stunning and surreal.**

Culinary Delights to Match the Scenery: **The menu at "The Glass Goose Bar & Eatery" is a treat in itself. Offering a range of delectable dishes and refreshing beverages, it's a spot where you can savor both the flavors and the sights. The ambiance is perfect for a romantic dinner, a get-together with friends, or simply a solitary escape where you can revel in the magic of cinema.**

These themed cafes and restaurants in New Zealand are more than just places to dine; they're destinations in their own right. They're settings that transport you into the world of movies, where art and food intertwine to create an immersive experience. Here, every meal is a journey through cinematic wonder, and every moment is an opportunity to appreciate the artistry of film from a fresh perspective.

Tasting New Zealand's Film-Inspired Dishes

New Zealand's cuisine is a reflection of its rich cultural heritage and the bounty of its stunning natural landscapes. While the allure of film-themed settings is undeniable, your journey isn't complete without savoring the local dishes that capture the essence of the land.

Traditional Maori Food Experiences: **Immerse yourself in the vibrant tapestry of Maori culture by indulging in traditional food experiences. The "hangi," a feast prepared in an earth oven, is a culinary adventure that allows you to experience the heart of Maori cuisine. Within the "hangi," you'll discover treasures like "kumara," the sweet potato that's a Maori staple; "rewena," the beloved Maori bread with a distinctive flavor; and "kina," a delicacy harvested from the sea, also known as the sea urchin. These dishes are not just food; they're windows into the history and soul of New Zealand's indigenous culture.**

Exploring Local Markets and Food Festivals: **As you journey through New Zealand, you'll find a tapestry of vibrant local markets and food festivals that celebrate the country's culinary diversity. These gatherings are a treasure trove of flavors and experiences, allowing you to sample fresh seafood, artisanal cheeses, and delectable street food. As you mingle with locals and fellow travelers, you'll discover a world of tastes that span from the sea to the mountains, from traditional recipes to contemporary fusions. These markets and festivals are more than places to eat; they're opportunities to engage with the pulse of New Zealand's gastronomic scene.**

In addition to the film-themed dining experiences, these culinary adventures open up a gateway to the authentic flavors of New Zealand. They invite you to journey through a diverse landscape of tastes, making your exploration of Middle-earth not only visually stunning but also a delight for your taste buds. It's a journey where every dish tells a story, and every bite is a celebration of the land's rich culinary heritage.

As you savor the culinary delights of New Zealand and explore film-inspired settings, you'll find that your senses are awakened by the flavors, aromas, and ambiance of this extraordinary land. In the following chapters, we'll delve into the thrilling outdoor activities and cultural experiences that will further enrich your cinematic journey through New Zealand. Whether you're a film enthusiast or a devoted foodie, your adventure continues to unfold in this magical realm of film and fantasy.

Chapter 6

Fantasy-Infused Activities

Beyond Film Sets: Adventure Awaits

The magic of Middle-earth extends far beyond the film sets, beckoning adventurers and fantasy lovers to explore the breathtaking landscapes that served as the backdrop for some of cinema's most iconic moments. In this chapter, we'll delve into the thrilling outdoor adventures, cultural experiences, and practical tips that will enhance your journey through the fantasy realms of New Zealand.

Outdoor Adventures in Middle-earth

New Zealand's remarkable natural beauty beckons you to step into your favorite fantasy tale, where the grandeur of the great outdoors becomes your playground. From hiking through awe-inspiring landscapes to experiencing the exhilaration of skydiving over the remarkable mountains, Middle-earth offers a smorgasbord of adventures that cater to every kind of thrill-seeker.

Hiking Through Otherworldly Landscapes: New Zealand is a hiker's paradise, boasting a network of trails that take you through landscapes that seem plucked from the realms of fantasy. Whether you're traversing the otherworldly terrains of the Tongariro Alpine Crossing, where volcanic peaks rise like ancient sentinels, or meandering through the enchanted forests of Fiordland National Park, you'll find that every step is a journey into a world of natural wonder. These trails lead to vistas that are so breathtaking, they seem like they've been painted by the gods themselves.

Skydiving Over Remarkable Mountains: **For those who seek thrills from high above, New Zealand is the ultimate destination for skydiving. Imagine plummeting from the heavens and free-falling over the rugged, snow-capped peaks of the Remarkables. The sensation of the wind rushing past you and the panoramic views of these towering mountains create a moment that's nothing short of euphoric. Your descent over Middle-earth is an adventure that blends exhilaration with awe, as you feel the heart-pounding excitement and absorb the astonishing beauty that surrounds you.**

Cultural Experiences for Fantasy Lovers: **In New Zealand, adventure isn't just about the outdoors; it's also about cultural immersion. For those with a love for all things fantastical, New Zealand offers unique cultural experiences. You can participate in cooking classes that unveil the secrets of traditional Maori cuisine or dance** to the rhythms of Maori performances. These cultural escapades not only transport you to the heart of Maori culture but also remind you of the rich tapestry of traditions that have inspired countless tales of fantasy.

Nightlife in Fantasy-Themed Bars: **The adventure doesn't conclude with the setting sun; it merely transforms. New Zealand's cities come alive at night with a nightlife that's as vibrant as it is unique. In these urban oases, you can find bars and nightclubs that pay homage to the worlds of fantasy and cinema. Sip on themed cocktails while being surrounded by memorabilia and decor that transport you into your favorite movies. These nocturnal adventures are a chance to let your hair down and celebrate the day's triumphs in a setting that's straight out of your most cherished stories.

New Zealand's outdoor adventures are more than just experiences; they're journeys into realms that inspire and captivate. Whether you're hiking through landscapes that seem born from dreams, taking to the skies to touch the mountaintops, immersing yourself in cultural traditions, or reveling in nightlife that feels like pure fantasy, your adventure in Middle-earth is a celebration of the extraordinary.

Hiking the Tongariro Alpine Crossing

Prepare yourself for an epic journey through the very landscapes that brought the fiery desolation of Mount Doom to life in "The Lord of the Rings." The Tongariro Alpine Crossing stands as one of New Zealand's most renowned hikes, a trail that offers an adventure that's both challenging and immensely rewarding. Here, you'll traverse otherworldly terrain, venturing past emerald lakes, steaming vents, and ancient lava flows as you immerse yourself in the fantastical landscapes of Middle-earth.

A Volcanic Wonderland: **The Tongariro Alpine Crossing isn't just a hike; it's an expedition through a volcanic wonderland. As you embark on this adventure, you'll feel as if you've stepped onto the set of an epic fantasy film. The rugged terrain, with its craggy rocks and barren slopes, serves as a reminder of the destructive power that once consumed the land in the tale of Mount Doom.**

Emerald Lakes and Steaming Vents: **Along the way, you'll encounter natural wonders that seem straight out of a dream. The emerald lakes, nestled in craters of past eruptions, glisten like precious gems against the stark landscape. Steam vents hiss and sputter, a reminder of the ever-present volcanic activity that shapes this realm. It's as if you're wandering through the heart of a world** that's both serene and tumultuous, where the forces of nature are in a constant dance.

Ancient Lava Flows and Surreal Beauty: **The trail takes you through ancient lava flows, an arid expanse that feels like the surface of another planet. These flows bear the scars of centuries past, a testament to the tumultuous history of this region. As you traverse this surreal beauty, you can't help but marvel at the juxtaposition of the earth's violent past with the serene present.**

A Rewarding Challenge: **The Tongariro Alpine Crossing is a challenging hike, one that demands both physical endurance and mental fortitude. Yet, with each step, you'll be rewarded not only with breathtaking vistas but also with the satisfaction of conquering the very terrain that helped shape one of the greatest stories ever told. It's a journey that leaves you with a profound sense of achievement and an indelible connection to the cinematic landscapes that inspired the imaginations of millions.**

Immersing in the Fantastical Landscapes of Middle-earth: **As you hike through the Tongariro Alpine Crossing, you can't help but be drawn into the fantastical landscapes of Middle-earth. The sense of being in a realm where fiction and reality intertwine is palpable. You'll find yourself walking in the footsteps of hobbits and heroes,** exploring a world that once existed only in the minds of storytellers. It's an experience that transcends the ordinary, leaving you with memories that feel like chapters from your very own fantasy epic.

Exploring Fiordland National Park

A visit to Fiordland National Park is akin to stepping into the most enchanting dream. Here, nature unveils its most exquisite beauty, and you find yourself exploring the fiords of Milford Sound and Doubtful Sound, whose cinematic allure captured the hearts of moviegoers across the globe. As you journey through these pristine fiords, you'll bear witness to the majestic landscapes that defined the land of Middle-earth.

The Dreamlike Fiords: Milford Sound and Doubtful Sound are more than just geographical features; they are living poems written by the hand of nature. Here, towering cliffs of ancient rock plunge into the deep, creating a labyrinth of fiords that seem like passages to another world. The still waters of these fiords mirror the grandeur of the landscapes, inviting you to explore their depths and secrets.

Cruising Through Cinematic Beauty: To truly appreciate the magnificence of these fiords, you must embark on a cruise. As you glide through their serene waters, you'll be enveloped by an ambiance of tranquility that's almost ethereal. The fiords are alive with the sound of nature, where the only interruptions are the cries of seabirds and the soothing rush of waterfalls. It's a voyage into a realm where time seems to stand still.

Towering Waterfalls and Untouched Wilderness: **Fiordland National Park is a world where waterfalls tumble from heights that defy the imagination. Among them, Stirling Falls and Bowen Falls are notable, cascading from immense heights, their waters glistening in the soft light of the fiords. The untouched wilderness that surrounds you is a testament to the pristine nature of this land, with its lush forests, snow-capped peaks, and untamed shores.**

The Essence of Middle-earth: **As you explore Fiordland National Park, you can't help but feel that you're experiencing the very essence of Middle-earth. It's as if the magic of Tolkien's world has materialized before your eyes. The landscapes, with their stark cliffs and deep waters, mirror the tumultuous history of the One Ring. The serene wilderness that stretches as far as the eye can see reminds you of the untamed lands of the story. Each moment spent here is a brush with the world that stirred the imaginations of millions.**

Exploring Fiordland National Park is not just a journey; it's an odyssey through the splendor of nature at its most unspoiled. It's a chapter in your own tale, one that leaves you with memories of cinematic beauty that will linger in your heart long after you've departed from these dreamlike fiords.

Skydiving Over Remarkable Mountains

For those who dare to chase the ultimate adrenaline rush and are in pursuit of breathtaking, soul-stirring views, New Zealand is nothing short of a skydiving paradise. Picture this: you're suspended in the heavens, the earth beneath you a tapestry of awe-inspiring grandeur. The Remarkable Mountains unfold below, a dramatic range that played a pivotal role in "The Lord of the Rings" and "The Hobbit." As you leap from the aircraft, you plunge into a world where time stands still, and the wind whistles past you, while your senses are flooded with the sheer magnitude of the landscapes that stretch as far as the eye can see.

A Journey into the Skies: **The adventure begins with a climb to the heavens. You'll ascend in an aircraft that carries you to dizzying altitudes, the Remarkable Mountains growing smaller below. With every passing second, the anticipation builds, your heart races, and you can hardly contain the exhilaration that's about to unfold.**

The Rush of Freefall: **The moment of truth arrives, and you launch yourself from the aircraft. In that instant, you're a free spirit, plummeting through the sky at a speed that defies description. The adrenaline courses through your veins as the Remarkable Mountains rush up to meet you. It's a rush unlike any other, a sensation that's both terrifying and electrifying.**

Dramatic Panoramas Unveiled: **As you freefall, the Remarkable Mountains come into sharp focus. Their rugged, snow-capped peaks and sweeping valleys create a landscape that's nothing short of epic. It's like being part of a living canvas, a world where the grandeur of nature knows no bounds. The cinematic beauty of this place is unlike anything you've ever witnessed.**

The Tranquil Unveiled Amidst the Thrill: **Amidst the thrill of freefall, there are moments of tranquility. When the parachute is deployed, the pace slows, and you find yourself suspended, as if in a dreamscape. The Remarkable Mountains are there, stretching in all directions, but now you have the luxury to soak in the beauty at a more leisurely pace. The world is vast, and you're a solitary speck amidst its enormity.**

An Adventure of Epic Proportions: **Skydiving over the Remarkable Mountains is an adventure of epic proportions. It's a dance with the elements, an** exploration of the skies, and a communion with the grandeur of the Earth. The sensation of wind rushing against your skin and the sheer velocity of the descent are unforgettable. The vistas, with the Remarkable Mountains as the star attraction, etch themselves into your memory.

The Essence of Middle-earth: **In these fleeting moments, you touch the very essence of Middle-earth. The Remarkable Mountains, with their stark beauty and towering majesty, evoke the landscapes that captured the imaginations of countless readers and viewers. It's as if you've been given a glimpse into a world where fantasy and reality intertwine.**

A Memory to Treasure: **Skydiving over the Remarkable Mountains is not just an adventure; it's a memory to treasure for a lifetime. It's a story you'll tell, a tale you'll relive, and a moment that will always be a part of you. The thrill of the experience is incomparable, and the vistas are nothing short of magnificent. It's a chapter in your own personal odyssey, where you become a part of the cinematic landscapes that once existed solely in the realm of fiction.**

Cultural Experiences for Fantasy Lovers

Beyond the breathtaking natural wonders that New Zealand offers, there's a treasure trove of cultural experiences waiting to be explored. These experiences provide a unique opportunity for fantasy lovers to immerse themselves in the rich and vibrant culture of this land. It's a chance to discover the traditions of the indigenous Maori people, witness captivating cultural performances, and actively participate in traditional Maori workshops. In New Zealand, the heart of Middle-earth beats not only in its landscapes but also in the pulsating rhythm of its people's heritage.

Maori Traditions Unveiled: **To** delve into the world of Middle-earth, it's essential to understand and appreciate the culture that inspired it. The Maori people, with their deep-rooted traditions and profound connection to the land, offer a gateway to this world. Through cultural experiences, you can immerse yourself in Maori customs, gaining insights into their values, beliefs, and unique way of life. It's a journey into a realm where the echoes of the past resonate in the present.

Captivating Cultural Performances: **One** of the most enchanting ways to experience Maori culture is through captivating cultural performances. These performances are a symphony of song, dance, and storytelling. The haka, a powerful ceremonial dance, is a highlight of these shows. The performers, adorned in traditional attire, mesmerize with their rhythmic movements and chants. It's a window into the spirit of the Maori people, a connection to the very essence of Middle-earth.

Traditional Maori Workshops: **For a hands-on immersion into Maori culture, traditional workshops are an invaluable experience. These workshops offer a chance to learn traditional Maori crafts and skills. You can try your hand at carving, weaving, and even the art of storytelling. It's a way to connect with the artistry and craftsmanship that are hallmarks of Maori culture, and by extension, the culture of Middle-earth.**

A Journey to the Heart of Middle-earth: **Cultural experiences in New Zealand allow you to embark on a journey to the heart of Middle-earth. It's a world where tradition and storytelling take center stage, where the land is not merely a backdrop but an integral part of the narrative. Through these experiences, you gain a deeper understanding of the profound connection between the people of New Zealand and the landscapes they inhabit.**

The Pulse of a Living Fantasy: **Cultural experiences in New Zealand infuse fantasy with life. They're not limited to mere observation; they encourage active participation. These experiences allow you to be a part of the living, breathing fantasy world that was inspired by the land and its people. It's a chance to touch, feel, and connect** with a realm that's usually confined to the pages of a book or the frames of a movie.

Creating Lasting Memories: The memories forged through these cultural experiences are enduring. They are more than just moments in time; they are chapters in your own personal odyssey. These experiences become a part of your own narrative, adding depth and color to your journey through Middle-earth. They transform your perception of the land and the tales it has birthed, making your adventure not just about places but about people and their rich cultural heritage.

Maori Cultural Performances

Immerse yourself in the enchanting world of Maori cultural performances, where the heartbeat of ancient legends and traditions resonates through every movement and melody. These performances are a gateway to a realm where time dissolves, and you are transported into the heart of New Zealand's indigenous heritage. The experience is a tapestry woven with powerful haka dances, melodious waiata (songs), and the intricate poi dances that collectively celebrate the rich and vibrant Maori culture.

The Power of the Haka: Central to Maori cultural performances is the haka, a ceremonial dance of indomitable strength and emotion. Performed with fierce determination, the haka is a profound expression of respect, challenge, and unity. The rhythmic stomping, aggressive postures, and haunting chants convey a depth of feeling that is both awe-inspiring and humbling. It's a direct connection to the warrior spirit of the Maori people and their inseparable bond with the land.

Melodious Waiata: As the haka reverberates, it is complemented by the melodious waiata, songs that fill the air with the magic of Maori storytelling. These songs weave tales of love, legends, and lament, often accompanied by traditional instruments like the guitar and ukulele. The waiata evoke a sense of nostalgia, a deep-rooted connection to the past, and a profound reverence for the land's history.

Intricate Poi Dances: Poi dances add a graceful contrast to the power of the haka. Performed with dexterity, poi dancers twirl weighted balls attached to cords, creating a mesmerizing visual spectacle. The intricate choreography showcases the skill and precision that is a hallmark of Maori artistry. The poi dances are a celebration of life's rhythms, an invitation to join in the cadence of a vibrant culture.

A Connection to the Land and History: Maori cultural performances offer more than just a visual and auditory feast; they create a profound connection to the land and its history. The narratives told through dance and song are deeply entwined with the landscapes and legends of New Zealand. It's a reminder that this land, with its soaring mountains, lush forests, and winding rivers, has been the backdrop for countless stories and struggles.

An Experience of Unity and Respect: **Attending a Maori cultural performance is an experience of unity and respect. It's an opportunity to honor the indigenous people of New Zealand and their enduring cultural legacy. The performers, adorned in traditional attire, become storytellers and custodians of their heritage, inviting you to share in their world. It's a testament to the power of culture to bridge gaps and transcend boundaries.**

A Profound and Unforgettable Connection: **Maori cultural performances leave an indelible mark on your journey through Middle-earth. They are not mere shows; they are bridges that connect you to a world where the past, present, and future converge. The performances transport you through time, allowing you to touch the essence of the land and its people, creating a connection that will stay with you long after the final note is sung and the last movement is danced.**

Traditional Maori Workshops

Delve into the heart of Maori culture by participating in traditional workshops that offer a hands-on connection to age-old customs. These workshops are an invitation to unlock the secrets of Maori artistry, where you can learn the ancient art of wood carving, master the intricate skills of weaving, or try your hand at crafting Maori jewelry. These immersive experiences are a profound way to connect with the culture on a deeper level, not merely as an observer, but as an active participant.

The Art of Wood Carving: **Maori wood carving is an expression of ancestral stories, spiritual connections, and intricate craftsmanship. In workshops, you'll have the chance to work with native woods and chisels to create your own carvings. You'll be guided by skilled artisans who pass down the techniques that have been honed over generations. The process is both meditative and awe-inspiring, as you bring to life your own piece of Maori art.**

The Magic of Weaving: **Weaving is an integral part of Maori culture, used to create functional items as well as intricate artworks. In weaving workshops, you'll learn the techniques and traditions that are woven into Maori life. From making traditional baskets to crafting decorative wall hangings, you'll gain an appreciation for** the skill and patience required to create these beautiful pieces.

Crafting Maori Jewelry: **Maori jewelry is known for its distinctive designs and symbolic meanings. Participating in workshops allows you to create your own piece of Maori jewelry, such as a bone pendant or a greenstone necklace. You'll explore the significance of these ornaments and their role in Maori culture while crafting a unique souvenir that carries a piece of Maori heritage with it.**

Creating Meaningful Souvenirs: **Beyond the artistry and techniques, these workshops offer you the opportunity to create meaningful souvenirs. These are not mere trinkets; they are reflections of your journey into Maori culture. Each piece you craft becomes a tangible connection to the land, its people, and their traditions. These souvenirs hold the stories of your own experiences, making them cherished mementos of your time in Middle-earth.**

A Deeper Cultural Connection: **Traditional Maori workshops offer more than just the chance to create art; they create a deeper cultural connection. You learn about the values, symbolism, and history that inform Maori art forms. It's a way to understand the spiritual** significance of each creation and how it weaves into the larger tapestry of Maori culture.

A Journey of Discovery: Participating in these workshops is not just an artistic endeavor; it's a journey of self-discovery. It's a path into the heart of Middle-earth's cultural landscape, where art becomes a bridge between worlds. The creations you fashion are not merely objects; they are gateways to the stories, beliefs, and beauty of the Maori people, making your journey through New Zealand an artistic and cultural odyssey.

Nightlife in Fantasy-Themed Bars

As the sun dips below the horizon and your day of enchanting adventures in New Zealand's Middle-earth comes to a close, there's no better way to wind down than by exploring the realm of fantasy-themed bars. These unique establishments are a portal to a world where movie magic and immersive experiences take center stage. Adorned with memorabilia from beloved films, they provide a cozy and welcoming atmosphere, inviting you to unwind and create lasting memories with fellow travelers. Whether you're sipping creatively crafted cocktails inspired by Middle-earth or enjoying a pint in a setting that evokes the magic of cinema, the nightlife in these bars offers a delightful conclusion to your day.

The Magic of Memorabilia: **Step into these fantasy-themed bars, and you're immediately transported to the heart of cinematic wonder. The walls are adorned with iconic memorabilia from beloved films, creating an ambiance that's nothing short of magical. You'll find yourself surrounded by familiar artifacts, from movie posters to life-sized character figurines. The bars are like treasure troves of cinematic history, offering a sense of nostalgia and enchantment.**

Cozy and Welcoming Atmosphere: **The atmosphere in these bars is cozy and welcoming, making them the perfect places to relax and reflect on your day of adventure. Soft lighting, comfortable seating, and a friendly, communal vibe set the stage for memorable encounters and captivating conversations. It's a space where travelers come together to share their experiences, swapping tales of their journeys through Middle-earth.**

Crafted Cocktails and Creative Concoctions: **The bars offer a menu of creatively crafted cocktails that pay homage to the fantastical worlds of cinema. Sip on beverages inspired by Middle-earth, each with its own unique twist and flair. From elixirs that evoke the landscapes of New Zealand to concoctions named after beloved characters, these cocktails are a delightful way to celebrate your love for both film and fantasy.**

A Pint in a Magical Setting: **For those who prefer the classic charm of a pint, these bars also offer an authentic experience. Enjoy your favorite beer or cider in a setting that's nothing short of magical. The bars are designed to evoke the ambiance of famous film scenes, making you feel like you've stepped into the heart of a beloved movie. It's a unique fusion of cinematic charm and conviviality.**

Creating Lasting Memories: **The nightlife in these fantasy-themed bars is not just about drinks; it's about creating lasting memories. It's a space where travelers from all corners of the world come together, united by their love for film and their shared journey through New Zealand's Middle-earth. These bars are places where stories are swapped, friendships are forged, and the magic of cinema lives on.**

A Night of Magic and Imagination: **A night in a fantasy-themed bar is a night of magic and imagination. It's a fitting conclusion to your day of exploring the landscapes and locations that inspired some of the most beloved films in cinematic history. These bars offer a bridge between the world of fantasy and reality, making you feel like a character in your very own adventure. Whether you're toasting to new friendships or simply** savoring the moment, the nightlife in these bars is an experience you won't soon forget.

As you venture beyond the film sets and into the world of outdoor adventures and cultural experiences, you'll find that New Zealand's enchantment knows no bounds. Your journey through Middle-earth is a tapestry of thrilling escapades and cultural immersion, where every moment is a page in your own epic tale.

In the following chapter, "Chapter 7: Safety and Practical Tips," we'll provide you with essential information to ensure a safe and seamless exploration of New Zealand's film and fantasy landscapes. Whether you're a thrill-seeker or a culture enthusiast, your adventure in Middle-earth continues to unfold.

Chapter 7

Safety and Practical Tips

Navigating Middle-earth Safely

As you embark on your journey through New Zealand's film and fantasy landscapes, safety should be a top priority. This chapter provides essential information on local customs, cultural sensitivities, health concerns, safety precautions, and emergency contacts to ensure you navigate Middle-earth safely and responsibly.

Local Customs and Cultural Sensitivities

Respecting the local customs and cultural sensitivities of New Zealand is crucial for a positive and meaningful travel experience. Here are some tips to keep in mind:

Maori Culture: Maori culture is deeply rooted in New Zealand's identity. When visiting Maori communities or cultural sites, it's important to show respect. Follow the guidance of local guides and adhere to any cultural protocols or practices.

Greeting: The traditional Maori greeting is the hongi, a pressing of noses. While not required for tourists, it's a sign of respect if offered. A simple "Kia ora" (hello) and a smile will always be appreciated.

No Shoes Inside: In many Maori and Kiwi households, it's customary to remove your shoes before entering. Pay attention to whether this practice is followed and act accordingly.

Tikanga: "Tikanga" refers to customary practices and etiquette. Being aware of and respecting local tikanga is essential when interacting with Maori communities.

Health Concerns and Vaccinations

Before traveling to New Zealand, it's advisable to consider health concerns and necessary vaccinations:

COVID-19: As of my last knowledge update in September 2021, COVID-19 was a global concern. Check the latest travel advisories, entry requirements, and health safety measures related to COVID-19 for New Zealand.

Vaccinations: Make sure your routine vaccinations are up-to-date. Consult your healthcare provider or a travel clinic for specific recommendations on vaccinations needed for your trip.

Travel Insurance: It's highly recommended to have comprehensive travel insurance that covers medical emergencies, trip cancellations, and other unexpected events.

Healthcare Facilities: New Zealand has a high standard of healthcare. In case of medical emergencies, you can access medical facilities across the country. Keep a list of important medical contacts and your insurance details handy.

Safety Concerns and Emergency Contacts

Safety should always be a priority when exploring New Zealand's diverse landscapes:

Emergency Services: In case of emergencies, dial 111 for police, fire, or medical assistance. New Zealand's emergency services are highly responsive.

Outdoor Safety: If you plan outdoor activities like hiking, check weather conditions, inform someone about your plans, and carry essential gear. Be aware of the risks associated with outdoor adventures.

Water Safety: New Zealand's waterways can be unpredictable. Follow safety guidelines for activities such as swimming, kayaking, and boating.

Driving Safety: If you plan to drive in New Zealand, familiarize yourself with local traffic rules and road conditions. Drive on the left side of the road, and ensure you have a valid driver's license.

Crime: While New Zealand is generally safe for travelers, exercise common-sense precautions. Keep your belongings secure, be cautious in secluded areas, and avoid leaving valuables in plain sight.

Weather and Climate Information

New Zealand's weather can be variable, so it's essential to be prepared:

Seasons: New Zealand experiences opposite seasons from the Northern Hemisphere. Summer is from December to February, autumn from March to May, winter from June to August, and spring from September to November.

Weather Variability: The weather can change quickly, especially in regions with diverse landscapes. Be prepared for varying conditions and dress in layers.

Rainfall: Some regions, such as the West Coast of the South Island, receive heavy rainfall. Check the weather forecast and pack accordingly.

Mountain Safety: **If you plan to hike or explore alpine areas, be aware of mountain weather conditions, which can be severe.**

As you navigate Middle-earth safely, you'll have the peace of mind to fully immerse yourself in the cinematic beauty and cultural richness of New Zealand. In the concluding chapter, "Chapter 8: Conclusion," we'll recap your extraordinary journey through New Zealand's film and fantasy landscapes and provide additional resources to enhance your travel experience. Your adventure is nearing its conclusion, but the magic of Middle-earth lingers on.

Thomas Will

Chapter 8

Conclusion

Your Journey Through New Zealand's Film and Fantasy Landscapes

As you reach the final chapter of this guidebook, take a moment to reflect on the incredible journey you've undertaken through New Zealand's film and fantasy realms. From the rolling hills of Hobbiton to the majestic fiords of Fiordland, you've explored the very landscapes that captured the imagination of filmmakers and audiences alike. Your adventure has been a tapestry of cinematic wonder, outdoor exploration, cultural immersion, and unforgettable moments.

Capturing the Magic: Creating Lasting Memories

Your journey through Middle-earth has been a tapestry woven with moments of awe and wonder. Whether it's the breathtaking beauty of a sunrise over the Remarkable Mountains, the taste of a hearty Hobbiton meal, the rhythmic power of a Maori haka, or the heart-pounding thrill of skydiving over iconic film locations, these are the memories that will stay with you forever.

They are the treasures you carry home, the stories you recount, and the magic that lingers in your heart.

A Travel Journal of Wonders: To ensure these memories remain vivid and everlasting, consider keeping a travel journal or diary. This journal will be your canvas to paint your adventures, to capture the emotions, sights, and sounds that have colored your journey. Include sketches, photos, and personal reflections. Let the pages breathe with life, filling them with the essence of your experiences. Each entry becomes a testament to the incredible tapestry of your time in New Zealand's film and fantasy landscapes.

Sharing Your Story: The joy of travel is not just in the experiences themselves but in the stories we share with others. As you recount your adventures, you become a storyteller, a guide to the magical world of Middle-earth. Share your experiences with fellow travelers you've met on the road, with friends and family eager to hear about your journey, and with those who dream of embarking on their own adventures. Your stories become a bridge, connecting others to the enchanting landscapes you've explored.

Reliving the Magic: The magic of your journey doesn't end when your feet touch familiar soil. It lives on in your memories, in the tales you tell, and in the photographs you've taken. As you flip through your travel journal or share your photos, you'll find yourself transported back to the heart of Middle-earth. The emotions, the beauty, and the sense of wonder will come flooding back, allowing you to relive those moments of enchantment.

Inspiring Others: **Your journey through New Zealand's film and fantasy landscapes can be an inspiration to others. Your tales and photos can ignite the spark of wanderlust in those who dream of their own adventures. Your experiences become a beacon, guiding others to explore the magical destinations you've uncovered.**

A Treasure Trove of Memories: **The memories you've gathered are more than fleeting moments; they are treasures. They are the intangible riches that enrich your life and shape your perspective. They are the proof that you've ventured beyond the ordinary, tasted the extraordinary, and lived the magic of Middle-earth. Your travel journal is the key to unlocking these treasures, preserving them, and sharing them with the world.**

A Testament to Your Journey: **Creating lasting memories is not just about witnessing spectacular landscapes or participating in thrilling activities; it's about your journey, your unique experience in Middle-earth. Your travel journal is a testament to your path, your** discoveries, and the personal growth you've undergone. It's a reminder that every adventure leaves an indelible mark on your soul.

In the End, It's About the Magic: **In the end, your journey through New Zealand's film and fantasy landscapes is about the magic. It's about the moments that have left you in awe, the experiences that have enriched your life, and the memories that will stay with you forever. Your travel journal is the enchanted scroll that holds this magic, preserving it for all time.**